GOING BANANAS

GOING BANANAS

compiled by

Charles Keller

illustrated by Rodger Wilson

Prentice-Hall, Inc. Englewood Cliffs, N.J.

3

Copyright © 1975 by Charles Keller
Illustrations copyright © 1975 by Rodger Wilson

Printed in the United States of America •J

Prentice-Hall International, Inc., London
Prentice-Hall of Australia, Pty. Ltd., North Sydney
Prentice-Hall of Canada, Ltd., Toronto
Prentice-Hall of India Private Ltd., New Delphi
Prentice-Hall of Japan, Inc., Tokyo

Library of Congress Cataloging in Publication Data
Keller, Charles.
        Going bananas.
        SUMMARY: Jokes told in the form of
conversations are illustrated with cartoon characters.
        1. Wit and humor, Juvenile. [1. Joke books.
2. Wit and humor]   I. Wilson, Rodger, 1947–
illus.   II. Title.
PZ8.7.K42Go   [817]   74–20906
ISBN 0–13–357772–4

10   9   8   7   6   5   4   3   2

FOR BAYARD AND COBY,
PAUL AND JACQUELINE

5

GOING BANANAS

9

10

11

12

13

14

15

17

18

19

20

21

22

25

27

29

31

35

38

41

42

43

44

46

47

49

51

59

60

65

66

67

69

71

72

73

74

78

79

80

81

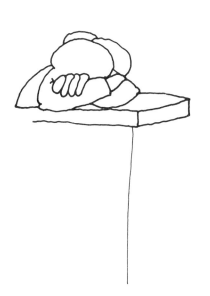

83

84

87

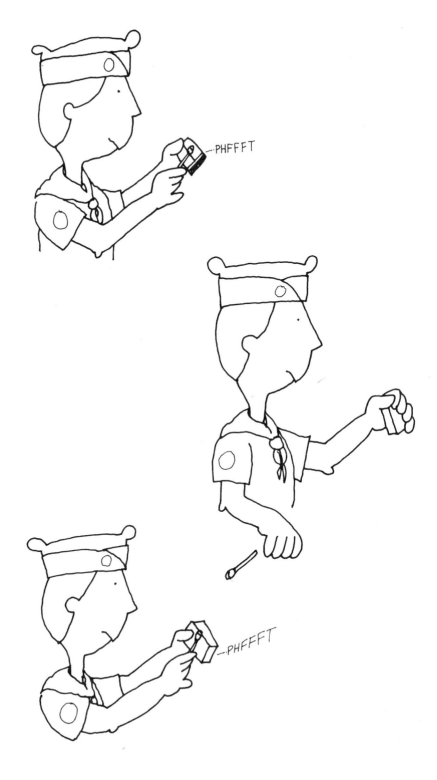

92